CLASSIC

GREENWICH STYLE

CLASSIC

GREENWICH
STYLE

CINDY RINFRET

FOREWORD BY
BUNNY WILLIAMS AND JOHN ROSSELLI

RIZZOLI
NEW YORK

First published in the United States of America in 2006
by UNIVERSE PUBLISHING
A Division of Rizzoli International Publications, Inc.
300 Park Avenue South
New York, NY 10010
www.rizzoliusa.com

© 2006 by Cindy Rinfret

2007 2008/ 10 9 8 7 6 5 4 3 2

Designed by Abigail Sturges
Printed in China

ISBN: 0-8478-2846-8
ISBN 13: 9-780-8478-2846-3

Library of Congress Control Number: 2006921639

Contents

Foreword

Greenwich, Connecticut, is a town from a dream. It is a suburban landscape containing many beautiful traditional homes built over a period of time. Cindy Rinfret has produced a very special book that allows the visitor to enter a warm, elegant, livable home. Cindy has an incredible eye for furniture and color, and each home is wonderfully planned both for the comfort of a family and for entertaining. Cindy's mixture of styles and textures creates rooms that will stand the test of time and become classics.

Bunny Williams
John Rosselli

Introduction

*G*REENWICH IS MORE than a charming town in southern Connecticut with a main street worthy of a Norman Rockwell painting, close proximity to horse country, and breathtaking views of Long Island Sound. More than almost any other community in America, Greenwich has come to signify a lifestyle, a way of living, and a state of mind.

No matter where I travel in the world, when asked where it is that I call home, I simply reply "Greenwich." There is no need to attach it to something larger, as Greenwich stands on its own with a simple yet unique identity, and a style that sets it apart from the rest of the world. Greenwich and its homes are aged and comfortable like a great pair of jeans, but at the same time command the classic elegance and timelessness of a beautiful cashmere sweater.

This book is not about a place but about a style that remains fresh and relevant today while also showing tinges of the history that has cultivated its vibrancy and richness. Greenwich is one of the most exclusive and desirable communities in America. It maintains this distinct style without succumbing to the trends that so quickly change society and disappear soon after. Greenwich style is a constant, controlled by a standard of beauty and luxury that demonstrates a life well lived and homes with furnishings that are meant to be lived in. A true Greenwich home is not a stage set with traditional furniture that fills a room; it is instead an inviting and comfortable environment created for a modern family.

Imagine long, winding gravel driveways leading past stone gates to magnificent homes, reminding those who live there of the rich past that has built what exists in Greenwich today. There is a history and depth to the architecture dating back to 1640, when Greenwich was founded as a small colonial village. Today some of the most magnificent estates have been created there by some of America's finest architects, although careful attention has been paid to remain faithful to Greenwich's traditional beginnings.

For the last twenty years I have had the pleasure of designing some of the most magnificent residences on the East Coast: homes that reflect endurance, elegance, and a refined lifestyle for the people who live in them. The houses exude the confidence of their owners while suggesting legacies of the past and new traditions for the future. The interiors I design reflect well-placed values and welcome friends and family with an air of warmth, generosity, and grace. Greenwich style means built for forever. It is meant for generations of children and holidays to be shared under one roof, unchanging in its relevance even while those within the walls grow and change.

I am Connecticut born and raised but returned to Greenwich after attending the Rhode Island School of Design and apprenticing in New York as a designer for many years. When I decided to start a family I thought, like many people, of Greenwich. To me, it is the ultimate "Town and Country": close enough for my city-fix when needed, but a perfect place to raise my children and three dogs. I opened my first shop in 1990, importing decorative accessories from England. I had always dreamed about having a shop like the ones on Walton Street in London with my studio nearby. It satisfied my two passions: one for interior design and the other for traveling. The shop gave me the opportunity to travel all over the world and bring back treasures both to use in my design business and to make available to the public. When I opened my first shop, a small storefront that looked like an English Mews house, my very first client was a charming young woman, the wife of fashion designer Tommy Hilfiger. Needless to say, it was not a bad start for the fledgling designer in town. Susie Hilfiger loved anything English, and I have since worked on more than nine homes for the Hilfigers. My business has grown over the years. The store is now much larger and located on Greenwich Avenue, the "main street" of Greenwich. My clients are gracious and indulgent of my passion for detail and design.

So what is the essence of Greenwich style? First, I believe it is necessary to allow what is outside to guide how the interior is designed. The home should be viewed as a package, from the beginning of the driveway to the last book on the bookshelf. Style allows you to choose how your life is presented, and, conversely, the life you create is reflected in the essence of your home. It is not about trends but about how you want to live. From the entry to your home to the children's playground in the yard, each aspect of your home should make a statement of good judgment and timelessness. My own children's outdoor play area has a box-wood walkway and private garden. It fits into the landscape and has given all of us fabulous memories. We even decorated and swagged it for Christmas.

I also believe that interesting rooms combine furniture of different styles and periods. Each object does not have to be important and precious but should contribute to the ambiance of the room and make it comfortable and inviting. There is nothing more unappealing than a gorgeous room that is untouchable and therefore left unused and unlived in. Greenwich style is about livable comfort for family life without sacrificing beauty and stylishness.

Last, and perhaps most important, I don't believe in design that is trendy or timely, or that will become dated. I strive for a look that is enduring. A beautiful piece of furniture, not pegged to any trend, was pleasing twenty years ago and will be pleasing twenty years from now. Just as furniture can be timeless, so can the design of a home. No matter how many years pass, the design will still be appropriate.

Greenwich style may have grown out of a look that is associated with the town and the houses in it, but its philosophy may be used anywhere. My approach is by definition universal, as it always centers around the lifestyle of a family, and takes into consideration both appearance and functionality.

What follows is a selection of some of the homes I have designed in or around Greenwich—in town, off the Sound, in the country—as well as a home or two located elsewhere but decorated in the tradition of Greenwich style. My hope is that once you enter the Greenwich world you will feel as much at home here as I do.

Timeless Tradition

Traditional and stately homes have come to be synonymous with the word "Greenwich." The three houses that follow are very different from one another, but they all share a common tradition: a focus on family life and entertaining. Rooms are decorated to display elegance and style, yet can easily accommodate the daily activities of children.

A Greenwich Classic

OWN A WINDING ROAD in Greenwich's mid-country section sits a home that is pure Greenwich style. While the house appears to have been on the site since the 1930s, it was built only a few years ago. In designing and constructing the home, the designers and builders paid painstaking detail to make sure it felt as if it were in the proper era in a neighborhood that contains some of the most impressive homes in Greenwich. In short, in its character and quality, the house is classically Greenwich.

When you open the mahogany front door, you feel inspired by the intricate inlay floor. The entry has no windows; nor was there a logical spot for a rug. My job was to make the entry dramatic and interesting; after all, it is the first impression a visitor has of the house. So I created a faux-bois parquetry floor. I worked with the artist Nels Christianson, a good friend, to create the layout and patterns. Nels and I met in Belgium years ago, and we have been working together ever since.

The vestibule ahead of the entry was designed with a rosette within an inlay border, which mirrored the light fixture over the center of the rosette. In the foyer the pattern was changed to a different scale. The use of a multi-tone wood floor to represent a reclaimed antique inlay floor carries through the central part of the house. It dresses the first floor and provides a magnificent view when you are descending the stairs from the second floor. The floor sets the tone for the entire home.

Right and opposite: The library has a secret door with faux books that opens onto a bar/sitting room, perfect for entertaining.

Below: The powder room was designed around a bamboo chest found in England.

This entry has just the right pieces, such as an eighteenth-century chinoiserie clock, unusual in its golden coloring. A gilt and marble console balances the importance of the floor and makes the entry exciting without competing with the parquetry.

I never overlook powder rooms. If decorated properly, they can be very memorable. Here the powder room is a real jewel. I had been on a buying trip to London when I found a spectacular bamboo chest. I bought it, not knowing where it might end up. As I was working on the house, I realized the powder room was the perfect size for this chest. I added a stone top, faucets, and a sink.

I designed a wainscot detail based on the front panels of the chest and had Nels faux-paint the details over molding I had installed. Instantly, the dresser became a part of the room, not just an antique in a new space. I completed the thought by adding the same detail to the crown molding and ceiling. I upholstered the walls in a fabric the client had found and loved.

Left: In the family room, simple curtain panels are hung on mahogany-fluted poles with Gilt rings.

Above: A game table corner was designed with custom bookcases.

After weeks of hunting, I found a bamboo light fixture, tole ivy sconces, and an antique bamboo mirror; the room was then complete. It is one of my favorite spaces in the house; not a person goes into the powder room who is not struck by its charm. I give the client credit for allowing me the chance to realize my vision for the room and let my sense of detail be fulfilled.

Every home needs a library. For this library I chose honeyed pine paneling. The curtains are simple panels over bamboo shades. They filter the sun during the day, creating a warm light in the room. The mix of the mahogany-fluted poles and pine rings on the curtains adds to the layering effect. Toast-colored wood tassels were affixed to the curtains. The fabrics are linens, suede, chenilles—with a little tiger thrown in for fun. The tiger is used on a Chippendale chair, making it less grand. Greenwich style is just that—traditional, but with a twist, a splash of personality.

I designed a secret door with faux books that opens onto a bar/sitting room. A visitor does not know the library has anything other than bookcases until the host goes for a drink and slides away one of the shelf areas to reveal a doorway to the bar. I love the element of surprise in this design.

The sitting room is a great overflow space for when the owners are entertaining, especially because it contains a bar. The walls are covered in antiqued chinoiserie panels from Charles R. Gracie & Sons of New York. The tree and bird paper is a gorgeous background that creates a peaceful backdrop around a bay window looking onto the trees. The antique tray table and needlepoint pillows provide a special character to the intimate lounge area.

The living room has French doors that open to the outside. I gave the room an established quality by adding pilasters and a hand-carved walnut Georgian-styled mantel. The door treatments were important to the room. I did not want to hide the transoms on the door, so I added tailored swags over fluted poles with mahogany and gilt finials. The linen on the windows is tea-stained to give the appearance that it has always been there and was not decorated yesterday. The jabots on the swags were lined in a cranberry and sage linen plaid. The curtains were designed to give height and character to the room. They are simple yet elegant, tailored yet detailed; they become a prominent feature of the room.

The walls were glazed in a pale wheat color. The textured paint on the walls and molding prevents the room from feeling new; it appears as if it were original to the house. Ceilings need to be treated, not left white; a plain ceiling makes a room feel as if the builder has just left. The living room contains several excellent pieces, but one in particular takes your breath away. The chinoiserie secretary was designed and built for the room. I couldn't find an antique with the correct proportions and strength, so I had a secretary made in a dark tobacco color with a merlot interior. The pediment on the top gracefully meets the drapery finials. The secretary is set off by a gilt and sage Prince of Wales chair with a carved feather back. A rug, featuring a Regency box pattern, balances the floral in the room.

The mixture of periods, textures, and styles is what gives the room character. It has chinoiserie tables next to Regency, antiques alongside reproductions. The key is to create a space that displays good taste. Greenwich style is comfortable, unpretentious, and, above all, timeless.

The entry opens into the dining room. I added the antique mirror niche to the back of the room. I did not want the view to be of a blank wall; I wanted just the right piece of furniture, so I had the niche created and set an amazing console in it. The space can serve as a buffet or a place to display flowers for a dinner party. I placed lamps on the console; I love the glow of ambient light given off by the red crystal column lamps.

All of the walls were upholstered in floral linen from Benison Fabrics in London. The fabric has a slightly aged background to give it an ageless character. This is the room people get dressed up for—and celebrate in. The curtains are "dressed up" too, with fancy cords and tassels; however, all of the fanciness is balanced with a relaxed diamond sisal rug.

The client owned the dining table and side chairs, but they were undersized for the room. So I added two chairs. Instead of using the same chairs, I chose two upholstered chairs to place at the heads of the table. The curved shape of the armchairs adds volume and character. It feels as if the owners had acquired the furniture in the room over time instead of purchasing it all at once.

Opposite: The dining room receives warm light from the red crystal column lamps on the console.

Above: The table is set for a celebration.

The butler's pantry is a perfect place to store china, stemware, and dining accoutrements, and doubles as a bar for entertaining.

In the family room, my favorite area is the game table corner, which I designed using custom bookcases to create balance to the fieldstone fireplace that dominates the room. Originally, the corner was dead space. Now it is an ideal place to play chess or cards, or to work on the laptop.

A fine home needs a butler's pantry. Although most people do not have butlers today, the pantry is essential. It is a place to store china, stemware, and dining accoutrements that aren't used every day. Along with kitchen designer Christopher Peacock, I created a space in red lacquer with a tea-paper ceiling and cut-crystal bell-jar lanterns. The back of the pantry features an antique mirror to give it an aged quality. The room is as pretty as it is functional.

Christopher also helped me with the kitchen. The pilasters and fluting details feel natural to the house; the kitchen functions like a room, not just a kitchen. One of the client's requests was for a conservatory, so off the kitchen I created a space with a vaulted ceiling and two walls of windows with transoms to look out onto

Right: The breakfast room has comfortable chairs and a beautiful view of the garden.

Opposite: Pilasters and fluting details make the kitchen feel as detailed as the rest of the house.

the garden. The breakfast room is an enticing place to start the morning; the upholstered seats are comfortable enough to sit in all day.

Upstairs, there are three boys' bedrooms. When I design children's rooms, I try to make them functional enough to be appropriate as the children grow, but not too contrived. The first bedroom has green striped walls and a custom wood valance on the window. The British Colonial mahogany and cane bed complements the tartan plaid used in the room. The second bedroom features a scheme designed around a bed I had copied from a nautical antique bed I found; the bed was re-created with the son's name painted on the headboard. A painting of the America's Cup race hangs between the windows. A fabric with the nautical alphabet was used to create a duvet cover. A red flannel tufted chair and ottoman is a good place to sit and read. The drum lamp was found on one of my London buying trips. In the third bedroom, I designed the bed with a patriotic crest. The mix of mahogany and painted pieces

*Above and opposite: The boys'
bedrooms will continue to be
appropriate as the children grow.*

*Right: The master bedroom
is handsome yet romantic.*

keeps the room young but attractive. The bedrooms have similar elements but are strikingly different and comfortable for the young men of the house.

The master bedroom has wheat-colored walls. A custom hand-painted tester was designed to create a romantic retreat. The headboard is upholstered in Colefax & Fowler linen, which was used on the canopy and curtains. The dark brown rug grounds the color palette. This keeps the room handsome but feminine at the same time.

The clients' main request was for me to create a warm and inviting home—timeless, not trendy—tailored to accommodate their three boys. To me, this is Greenwich style. Rooms should look as if they have been there for years, not decorated yesterday; they should look as classic years from now as they do today. Greenwich style is an extension of the English philosophy that says you should not buy quantity but quality. If you buy what you love, regardless of the price, you will always be happy with it.

Provence on Pecksland

Above: The monogram used in the inlay reflects the melding of the wife's name with the husband's.

Opposite: The mantelpiece in the foyer features a seascape from the clients' collection.

HE MOMENT YOU TURN OFF Pecksland Road, one of the most stunning roads in Greenwich's mid-country, and hear the gravel crackling as you pull through the open gates, you sense you are going to be taken away to another place and time. As you approach the front courtyard, you can see the house has age and character. You are greeted by a wall fountain, which is an experience not only of visual beauty but of sound as well. The property is alive with the scent of cherry blossoms and lilacs. The tableau appears natural, but it's actually well thought out and crafted; nothing is left to chance. Imagine coming home every day to this house; it exudes warmth and comfort. When designing a home, it's essential to consider the outside as well as the inside. Decorating is not just about furnishing, but experiencing your life and defining how you want your life to feel.

When you enter the foyer, the monogram used in the inlay reflects the melding of two lives into one. The "W" stands for the husband's first name, the "M" the wife's. So the initials, intertwined in a unique monogram, symbolize the couple's union. One of the hallmarks of Greenwich style is making a home personal and lasting. This inlay—quietly done in faux bois, with three tones of wood—does just that.

Continue into the foyer and you discover the focal point is a mantelpiece featuring a seascape from the clients' collection. The subtle blues, yellows, and off-whites predict the colors that will be used throughout the house. The window seat is a quiet place to wait for arriving guests or for casual discussion. It looks out onto the back courtyard with its vine-covered pergola.

In the living room, the palette of garden colors reflects the scenery outside.

A combination of period furniture helps to create a collected look. Nothing should appear as a "matched set" but instead as "found" items that have been gathered together. As long as the scale works, a room's furniture can be enhanced by its differences. In the entry I used French chairs, an English dresser, lanterns, and chinoiserie garden stools and cachepots.

Greenwich style means having the confidence to mix furnishings and know that they will look good because you love what you have brought together. I adore a home where furniture or accessories can be moved from room to room and feel right anywhere. That effect is achieved in this house with a palette of garden colors. Like the outdoors, where a variety of colors seems to blend, so it is in the interior; the key is the balance that is attained.

Off the entry, a library features bleached oak with brass grillwork on the cabinets. The French doors open onto a terrace that is perfect for entertaining. The room has comfortable throw blankets, which can be used to cuddle up under while reading a book on the sofa. On

the shelves the books are mixed in with treasures and photographs. A collection of porcelain adorns the mantel and the room's tables. When you look out the French doors to the soaring hemlock trees that canopy the terrace, you realize the outdoor furniture is part of the scheme of the house. The monogrammed pillows are used inside and out, treating the terrace as a room. The almost invisible boundaries maximize the effect.

Entering the living room, you are taken by its serenity and charm. Again, the colors mimic the gardens outside; pinks are pulled out of the ornamental cherry trees into the pillows and accents in the room. The chintz was a favorite of the clients, as was the antique hand-colored Bestler prints on the walls. I decided to allow the windows to let the outside in, unobstructed by window treatments except in a quiet alcove for collections and a piano. The walls are done in pale, grass-green, sponge-on-sponge stripes to enhance the expansive lawns outside. Antique dishes, books, and photographs decorate the shelves and cocktail tables.

Open the doors to the garden courtyard and you are greeted by two inherited "ladies" that came with the house. They are attributed to Frederick Law Olmsted, who landscaped the estate next door. I assume this property was once a carriage house for a grand estate. Along with the "ladies," another lady was found covered up and hiding in overgrown boxwoods. I estimate that she may have been hidden there for fifty to sixty years. She was not found until the client uncovered her while gardening one day. When the gardeners trimmed the boxwoods away, the statue of Venus appeared.

The dining room was built around a collection of eighteenth-century decoupage-framed Charles Edwards English bird prints. The yellow, pink, and

Opposite: Leaving the windows unobstructed in the living room allows full views into the garden.

Above left: Curtains in the breakfast room have cherry trim and plaid linings.

Above right: Furnishings and accessories can be moved from room to room and feel right anywhere in this house.

Opposite: The dining room was designed around the antique Charles Edwards English bird prints.

Above: The master bedroom offers a peaceful retreat after a long day.

blue chintz floral curtains tie the colors of the house together and create a backdrop for the Royal Darby dishes and blue chinoiserie accessories. Candles are a must in a dining room. Here centerpieces are not flowers but boxwoods in cachepots. This room is magical when dining.

The kitchen, next to a family room, is a step away from a terrace on which breakfast can be served. Again, the space allowed the blending of the inside and outside. In the breakfast room, notice the attention to detail in the curtains, with their cherry trim and plaid linings. The drapery pole is art unto itself. An antique barometer fits perfectly on a corner wall. You can sit here for hours reading a newspaper or taking in the view.

Upstairs, the color scheme in the master bedroom underscores the owners' love of blue and white. The sky is brought into the room through the windows, which have a clear view between the trees. Monogrammed linens dress the bed. I adore monogrammed bed linens and exquisitely made beds. I believe the last place you go at the end of the day and the first place you wake up in the morning should be an oasis from a busy world. Here the loveseat at the foot of the bed offers a quiet seat in front of a fire. In the room there is evidence of the owners' passions: decoupage lamps, botanical prints, and flower arrangements.

Featuring monogrammed pillows, the terrace is treated as another room. Boundaries between outdoors and in are kept to a minimum.

The clients' love of color is seen in the two daughters' bedrooms as well. The younger girl has a charming dormer bedroom with window seats covered with pillows. A stuffed animal sits upon a chintz-tufted child's chair, carrying out the blue and red chintz theme. The crisp white bed linens are piped in blue and monogrammed. This is any little girl's dream room.

The teenage daughter has a four-poster bed glazed in celadon. Chintz was used on the bed's dust ruffle and in the curtains. On the bed is a down comforter that the family's King Charles spaniel has grown fond of and proudly has claimed as his own. A Warhol-style portrait is set against a tufted slipper chair. The colors in the teenage daughter's wardrobe complement the colors of her room.

Outside, the garage is not so much a garage as a "folly," something attractive to see as it orients the view, making it a part of the landscape. When is a garage not just a garage? When you add a cupola, weathervane, pleasing doors, and landscape. Then it becomes a kind of garden ornament. This can be done with any outbuilding, including playgrounds and pools.

Don't be afraid to make your home what you love. Don't make it what is fashionable at the moment; make it what will endure over time. *That* is Greenwich style.

A Stately Tudor

Above: The Chinese chest brightens the oak-paneled entry.

Opposite: Lanterns were custom-crafted to enhance the tall ceilings.

WHEN YOU TURN THE CORNER onto this Belgian-block, tree-lined driveway and see the house for the first time, you are stopped in your tracks. A majestic English-style manor built in the 1930s, the house is as handsome as it is intimidating. With its age and beauty, it feels as if it has a past, a history. The house's exterior, replete with arches and turrets, looks as if it should be in Europe, not New England. The whole image conjures up thoughts of the great estates in Scotland, or perhaps *Wuthering Heights*.

The house is reminiscent of the client's childhood home, a slate-roofed stone manor in Bronxville, New York. I was asked to transform an imposing old house into a home suitable for a growing family. The interiors needed to be lightened up, yet I had to preserve the character of the house. Because the client had a boy and a girl, both under ten, I needed to keep in mind that young children would be ever present. The architecture is so strong that the decorating had to balance and enhance it without becoming trite or cliché. I tried to create a home the family could grow into and feel comfortable in for years to come. After all, the house, grand but understated, had a sense of prominence and agelessness, as if it had always been there and will always be there—the very essence of Greenwich style.

The trees are full and towering, the gardens mature. The vast lawns and ample shrubs are impeccably groomed, but it is the Japanese red maple tree that dominates the upper part of the driveway and leads down the stone path to the front door. That door opens onto an oak-paneled entry. I retained the walls and the limestone floor

but brightened them with a Chinese chest. An Oriental rug, with gold and reds, supplies color and light. I had the lanterns custom crafted, using a gothic influence, to accentuate the entry's nine-and-a-half-foot ceilings. The entry may be serious in character, but the colors are lively and help to brighten the architecture.

On the entry staircase, I used a gold, russet, and red runner. A dramatic colorful window treatment, with large poles and gilded finials, balances the window's height and scale. This area needed fabric to warm up the glare and to muffle the limestone's echo.

The living room, with its arch-entry paneling, frames a large iron chandelier. Manor houses such as this one are dark because of the woodwork and because the windows are usually small in proportion to the rooms. As a result, proper lighting is vital. The framed entry paints a picture of the living room, and the eye is drawn to a leaded window draped in classic linen floral. The linen is used for its weight and texture, and the color brings life to what could be an intimidating space.

Step into the living room and you see it was designed with one goal in mind: to be lived in every day. The fabrics are chenille, velvet, and needlework—all durable—

Right: Elaborate curtains set against the simple plaid wall upholstery give the dining room warmth and elegance.

Below: Blue and yellow valences are used on the kitchen windows, allowing views to the outside.

Opposite: The fireplace in the kitchen is a natural gathering spot for the family.

so the room will hold up under the strain put on it by a family. The room can't simply be pretty; it has to survive the daily comings and goings of children and dogs. The client wanted a television in the living room, which is unusual for a formal setting, to make sure the space would be used as much as possible by the entire family.

The room's design, then, centers on function. The rug features a brown background and a russet ribbon pattern to "kick it up"; it feels young yet sophisticated. At the end of the room, a desk doubles as a sofa table, with lamps to read by. A pair of cabinets on stands was designed to flank the doorway but also to house the entertainment system. The painting over the fireplace gives life, color, and character to the limestone mantelpiece, while a pair of tall English wingchairs in ribbed velour stripe balance the mantelpiece's height and strength.

Off the living room, the library is a true "gem"—as in "gem" colors. The jewel colors of deep russet, green, and brown work with the book collection that lines the room. In fact, it was the books' bindings themselves that determined the room's palette. A sofa floats in front of one set of bookshelves, facing the fireplace, which is flanked by two chairs. The room's pine paneling has warmth and glow. I prefer pine libraries to dark ones; they are less formal and more inviting and understated. With its style, colors, and layout, the room beckons you to come in and stay.

Old books, cozy warm leather chairs, family photographs in attractive frames, silk shades, and reading lamps—these are just some elements of Greenwich style. The style is about character, not fashion, and this room is an excellent example. It would have been pleasing twenty years ago; it will still be appealing twenty years from now.

The paneling in the dining room presented certain issues. As splendid as the woodwork is, when twelve people gather for dinner at the table, the party noise can be deafening. Because of this, I upholstered the walls above the wainscots in a blonde linen plaid to give the room texture and warmth and to muffle sound. The room is almost a perfect square, so a round table was a must. The chairs, some of the best Regency chairs I've seen, were a present from the client's mother. Since

The russet, green, and brown bindings of the books are the inspiration behind the library's color palette.

the room is large with low ceilings, I had a chandelier made in proportion to the room. Instead of going "grand," I chose an iron and crystal fixture. I had the sideboard made with a marble top and gilt base to add glamour to the room and accommodate buffets. The curtains are like ball gowns with their silk tassels and rosettes. The mix of the simple plaid wall upholstery against the elaborate curtains shows the same confidence I love to have when getting dressed. It's like wearing jeans with a cashmere sweater and a Kelly bag—classic, elegant, always appropriate. The room is especially enchanting by candlelight.

In this house, the kitchen, with its pine paneling and stone floor, is the family's gathering place. The room's fireplace creates an appealing space to enjoy tea with a friend or to discuss homework with the children. Over the fireplace is an inlaid tile panel that becomes the room's focal point. The panel, like all of the room's furnishings, was imported from France. The tray table, sitting in front of the fireplace, was a found platter made into a table with a tray stand.

Everyone loves blue and white, and from the mantel to the breakfast dishes to the curtains, blue and white are used in the kitchen, along with yellow to enliven the space. Like the three-light iron chandelier, the iron drapery poles are a perfect complement to the leaded windows. The window treatments are detailed with contrasting plaid banding and lining. The plaid and wood trim with pine beads is ideal with the paneling. Curtain valances are utilized only on certain windows, and long pine shutters are hung on the leaded French doors, so none of the view to the exterior gardens would be obstructed. The kitchen opens onto a flagstone terrace that can be used for outdoor dining.

On the second floor, the master bedroom presented challenges. The paneling, as lovely as it is, has a strong presence, especially with the room's soaring ceilings. I upholstered the walls in a light tan, green, and brown chintz, and I treated the room like a "toile room." All of the walls, windows, and furniture are in one fabric. This is a way to soften the room and make all of the edges melt into one, which creates an elegant and unified feel in what could have been a difficult space. Standing in the room is like being inside a lined jewelry box.

Nearby are the children's rooms. So many times a client says to me, "Well, it's only the kid's room." But what in your life is more precious than your children? Also, if you give your child a place he loves, it encourages him to be proud of his surroundings. A lifelong appreciation of surroundings is important to cultivate even at an early age.

The house has two children's rooms—one for a boy, one for a girl. The girl's room was designed around the embroidered linen curtains. The weight of the fabric was ideal against the natural woodwork. In the room I mixed painted and wood pieces to create balance. A four-poster bed complements the room's high ceilings. A tole basket chandelier, found in London, gives the room warm light. Older homes tend to be short on lighting, so a center fixture was a must. The practicality of the room lies in the fact that it will work for a child from age six to sixteen. If a room is decorated with quality pieces, as this one is, it will stand the test of time—the first rule of Greenwich style.

The boy's room was richly paneled too. I lightened the area with a sisal rug and a linen animal-print fabric, also found in London. The room suggests a safari-adventurer theme. The sisal wing chair is traditional, but with a twist—it has a leather seat cushion. I love creating texture; I did so here by adding tortoiseshell matchstick blinds. Mixing the significant with the informal gives a look of confidence.

Before I was asked to decorate this house, it was too bold, too substantial. It was an ordeal to brighten the home while maintaining the architecture's integrity. I used linens and color to give the house life. I mixed reproductions and antiques to make sure the family could really live in the house. The clients love their home. They entertain often and use the place to great advantage. The clients were trusting in allowing me to take the house in the direction I felt would best fulfill their needs, and in the end we were thrilled with the results.

My inspiration behind the design came from the estates in Scotland, which are impressive because of their architecture and because they are actually used and lived in. That's part of their character; it's what makes them interesting. In the end my job was to create a home that, instead of being grand and imposing, could be loved and enjoyed by this family for many years to come.

Bedrooms were decorated with linens and color to brighten the dark paneling and soften the house's bold architecture.

Seaside Living

With the Long Island Sound just a breath away, Greenwich is home to some of the most enchanting views in the Northeast. The houses in this section were designed to bring the outdoors in, with rooms that take advantage of the scenery, objects that evoke a nautical theme, and colors chosen to reflect the sea. Whether grand or simply charming, these are truly rooms with a view.

Distinctively Bell Haven

The faux-bois nautical star, antique marble table, and hand-painted wall covering make the entry interesting and inviting.

The first time I saw this house was on the annual Antiquaries House Tour. It was a brilliant sunny day, and I remember thinking how breathtaking the view was as I stood on the house's porch and gazed out onto an astonishing view of the Greenwich shoreline. I am fortunate to see many great residences. There are very few homes about which I get a tinge of envy; this, however, was one of them. Many years passed. Then a stroke of good fortune—one of my clients bought the house and asked me to design it.

Greenwich's Bell Haven is a private community built around its shoreline. The homes are located on a peninsula that juts out into Long Island Sound. One of Greenwich's original neighborhoods, Bell Haven features a private beach and yacht club. The views are spectacular. But what's quaint about this grand neighborhood is its unanticipated informality. No one locks their doors, people walk in and out of one another's homes—it's a throwback to a kinder and gentler era.

When you arrive at the house's front courtyard, you are mesmerized by the view. The ever-changing seascape is captivating. Entering the house, you discover the foyer has a faux-bois floor created to imply a nautical star. In my travels I found an antique inlaid marble table with a carved base, which I used as the foyer's focal point. The table contrasts with the formal Chinese hand-painted wall covering with its silver leaf background. The mix is unique and surprising yet relaxed and inviting.

Since the house is integrated with the landscape, I once again brought the outside in with references to the gardens. A stone planter filled with seasonal

*Floral fabrics in the living room reflect
the tones of the seascape outside.*

flowers sits on the table. A crystal chandelier from Charles Winston of New York sparkles like the white-caps on the nearby tide. Mr. Winston passed away several years ago, much to the dismay of the decorating community. He was a true gentleman who had an eye for creating crystal chandeliers. (It must have been in his genes, for his brother, Harry, became a legend for cutting crystal of a different sort, diamonds.) In the foyer the combination of substantial pieces, such as the chandelier and wall covering, with the garden pieces makes the space original.

The living room features views of the water from all sides. The floral fabric has the same tones as the seascape and landscape outside. I carpeted the room with a patterned sisal matting, layering it with Aubusson rugs. The layering helps to underplay the importance of the antiques. What makes the living room exciting is the blend of styles, textures, and collections.

My client is a beautiful woman who loves collecting exquisite items. She has a timeless sense of style. So the room is filled with pieces she has gathered from around the world—Venetian chairs, a chinoiserie secretary and cocktail tables, French buillot side tables, and English

Below and right: The faux-painted library is warmly decorated with linen curtains, chenille brown and tan leopard sofas, and hand-embroidered damask pillows.

Above and opposite: The pine-paneled dining room is warmly lit by a Russian crystal chandelier.

decoupage lamps. The house has the feeling of always being added to, always changing, just like the sea upon which it looks.

Tucked under the staircase was a closet that had been used as a bar in the 1950s. I decided to mirror and lattice the space, then paint it the same color as the sea on a late afternoon—a deep teal blue. When the door is opened, the bottles, decanters, and mirrors all sparkle. It's magical.

Down two steps from the living room is a brilliantly detailed powder room. The client found a chinoiserie chest that I turned into a sink. My artist restored and lacquered the chest so it could be used as a basin. I designed the powder room around this one piece, with its black wainscot and bamboo chair rail. The frette work was hand-painted below the chair rail, and a border was hand-painted on the ceiling. All of the walls were covered in raffia. The Chippendale mirror fits between a pair of Venetian sconces. The blend of the precious and the common gives the room its richness.

I love designing powder rooms. You should take as much care designing a powder room as you do your living room. It's a small space, but, let's face it, everyone ends up there. It should be a "surprise" space to be discovered by your guests.

In the pine-paneled dining room I added an embossed gilt ceiling—again to produce a sense of layering and elegance. This client is glamorous and loves anything that sparkles. I had the paper created in San Francisco especially for the room. The warmth of the room glows under the gilded surface. A Russian crystal chandelier adds a touch of romance. The dining room chairs, already owned by

Right: The powder room was designed around a chinoiserie chest found by the client.

Below and opposite: A chinoiserie secretary is one of many exquisite pieces in the client's collection.

the client, were slipcovered with scalloped edges. I love "shopping" in this client's basement, as I'm always finding the best antiques there. She happened to have the perfect gilded table and rose medallion vases. The Venetian mirrors are a splendid introduction to the library beyond.

For the library I found a Beserabian rug at my favorite New York dealer, Hakimian. I had the room faux-painted by Nels Christianson. The room has striped tailored linen curtains with large wood beads and bamboo shades underneath. Two pine Blackamoors hold ferns and grace the French doors.

The English lantern fills the library with soft light. The sofas are upholstered in chenille brown and tan leopard with long bullion fringe. The scrubbed pine Venetian armchairs, with ball-and-claw feet, were bought at auction for the room. The linen pillows are from Benison in London; the damask pillows are hand-embroidered. No library should be without a fur throw to layer the arm of the sofa. Ultimately, the room envelops you with its warmth.

All the rooms in the house have a view of the water, including the bedrooms and study.

The guest cottage is warm and inviting.

Every room in this home has a view of the sea; the study is no exception. From the French writing desk, you can look out each window to the water. I think every home should have one dark room. This study has brown lacquered walls that come alive against the linen curtains and tortoiseshell blinds. Pattern upon pattern is used to complement the furniture and turn an unassuming room into an inviting place. The client's love of animal prints is seen throughout the home; here a chair is covered in Scalamandre tiger silk velvet.

On the second floor are two children's rooms. The son's room has a vestibule where I added a mono-grammed nautical star in faux bois. It introduces the room's nautical theme. A barley twist four-poster bed flanks a fireplace. The seagull perched on the mantel is similar to the real seagulls that often perch on the nearby window ledge. One of the characteristics of my designing is the belief that no ceiling should be ignored. In this room I painted the ceiling a deep blue-gray, suggestive of the daytime sky that can be seen from all of the windows.

The daughter's room has a bamboo four-poster bed. At the foot of the bed is a dressing table with mirrored crystal lamps; the silk pleated shades on the lamps are decorated with crystal and bamboo beads. The lamps flank a three-part painted antique mirror. The bed is sit-ting on an Aubusson rug over simple wool sisal carpeting.

Gracious living is essential to Greenwich style. Guest spaces are as consequential as any room in the house. They make a statement of who you are and how impor-tant your friends and family are to you. I take great care in decorating these rooms to make them extra-special and memorable.

There is a British Colonial feel to this guest cottage. The wing chairs are covered in a British hand-block linen. Blue and white porcelain is used throughout as a unifying element. Cut crystal bell jars hang between the coffers of the ceilings. The moment you enter this cottage you feel as if you have escaped to an island somewhere. You could stay there forever. A Greenwich-styled home welcomes you so warmly you never want to leave.

Carriage House by the Sea

The addition of decorative beams and an iron and crystal chandelier give the living room a sense of history.

$\mathcal{I}$ had always driven past this house and wondered what it looked like inside. Then one day I was sitting in my office when the telephone rang. The voice on the other end belonged to the woman who had just bought this rather worn, French-style carriage house located on property that has a remarkable water view. She wanted me to design the house I had wondered about for so long. I couldn't wait to walk through the place; I felt it was a diamond in the rough. When I got inside, I saw that years of renovation had taken their toll. My job was to give the house back its original character, and to improve it along the way.

The views of the water from the house were mesmerizing; they told me what needed to be done. Since the house was all about the vistas of the changing shore-line, I decided the colors inside needed to echo those that were outside. This was also a case of less being more. The house had to be understated, like a cottage on Nantucket or a farmhouse in Provence. I felt that a blend of American and European styles would work best.

I began by gutting the existing renovations to return the house to its skeleton. It was vital to get the proportions of the house right, so I enhanced the windows with decorative transoms. The living room windows were especially low. Because of the house's construction, I could not structurally raise the windows on one side without having to reframe the entire house; that was not a possibility. My solution was to create faux-mirrored transoms to coordinate with real ones elsewhere. This simple change made the proportions of the living room correct.

Right: Faux-mirrored transoms were created for the living room because the windows were low for the space.

Below: A limestone mantel was added for character.

Opposite: The river-rock fireplace in the family room reflects the walkways and seawall outside.

The living room had a tray ceiling, to which I added decorative beams. The beams gave the room character and integrity. They made the room feel as if it was original to the house rather than added on. The existing fireplace, poorly proportioned and made of fieldstone, was replaced with a limestone mantel, which changed the look and character of the room dramatically. I hung an iron and crystal chandelier in the center of the ceiling to make the room shimmer. The room now has a sense of history; it is quiet and subtle but reflective of the rich life that has been lived here.

Throughout the house, the colors reflect the sea—pale gray-blues, sand, and taupe. The many textures—linens, wood beads, iron, mahogany, bleached woods—feel as if they were collected or found on travels. The console in the living room reminds me of a garden gate with two urns, now lamps, resting on it. The curtains, on beautiful poles with wood beads, are tall and simple.

The step-down dining room opens onto a terrace overlooking a dock. The chairs, which were made for the room, are reminiscent of ship wheels. They fit with the scale of the room, which has a low-beamed ceiling. The color is a diamond-hued sisal that works well with the linen-colored, French-ship toile fabric I used for the curtains.

Opposite: The breakfast room was designed around the iron and leaf lantern.

Left: The faded browns and grass greens in the master bedroom reflect the outdoors.

I love the breakfast room. I found the iron and leaf lantern around which I built the room. I used linen, as I did through the rest of the house, because the stucco walls needed to be balanced with fabrics that have weight and texture. In the breakfast room, a French toile in blue and brown was the right selection, especially with the client's existing table and French chairs.

The family room has a dominant river-rock fireplace. It worked well in the house because the outside grounds have pebble walkways and a rocky seawall. The pine furniture is marvelous and relaxed with the stone.

Upstairs, the master bedroom has a fabulous view of the sea. I created a romantic white linen bed with a half-canopy. The tester was custom-designed to give the bedroom height and character. The colors are reflective of the outdoors—sand, faded browns, and greens like the sea grass outside. The mix of mahogany furniture, alabaster lamps, and painted pieces creates a dreamy and relaxed bedroom retreat.

There is something romantic about a carriage house. When thinking about the architecture of a house like this one, it's important to remember where the house is—its location. Here location is defined almost completely by the house's proximity to the sea. There is nothing pretentious about this house. You don't have to overdecorate if the architecture is right. Go with the positives of a house. Sometimes what you don't put in a house is as critical as what you do.

In the early evening, with the candles lit and the chandelier on, the house twinkles like the tide at sunset. It looks just the way I wanted it to look.

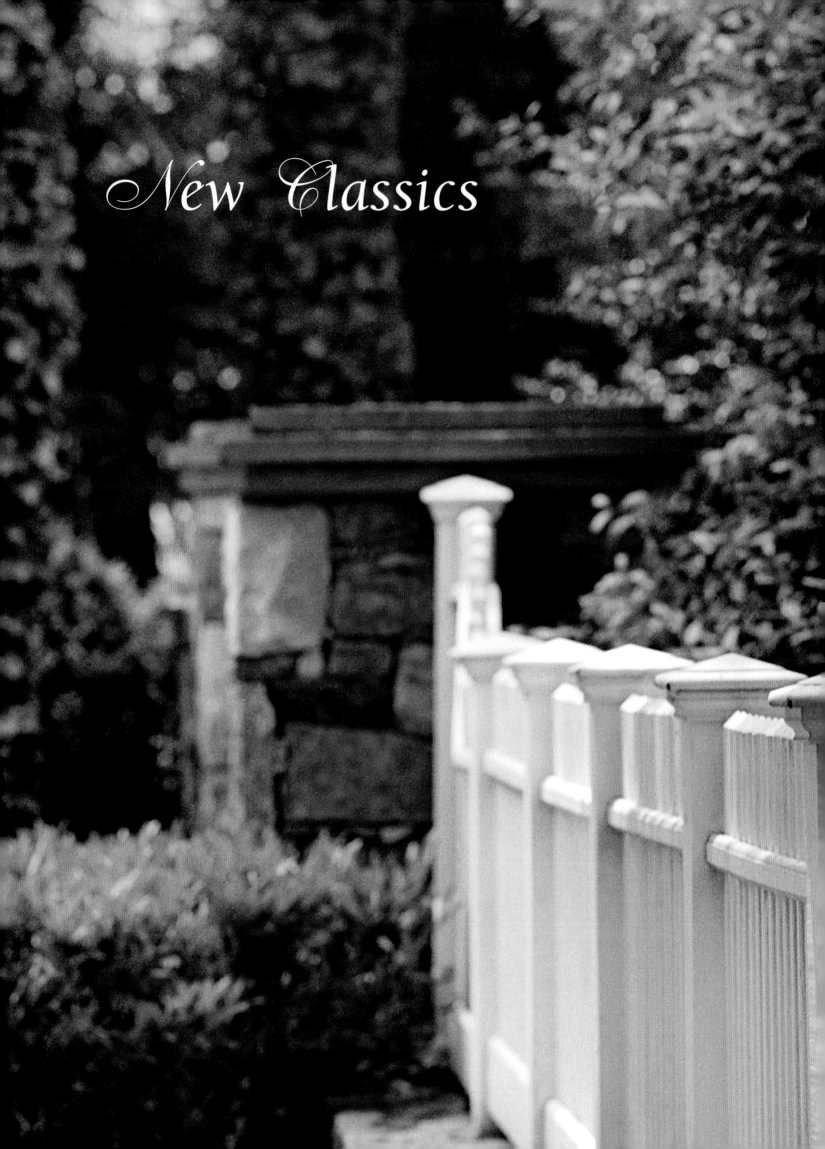

New Classics

The homes that follow are graciously inspired by the past with all the comforts of the present. They are a warm blend of contemporary materials with traditional forms; antiques alongside reproductions; valuable pieces and family heirlooms. These homes may be just a couple of decades old, but they reflect a character and quality that stand the test of time.

Classic Round Hill

A secretary sits at the end of a hallway lit by bell-jar lanterns and arched windows.

Situated atop Round Hill Road, one of Greenwich's highest points, this house has views that seem to stretch forever. To reach the classic brick Georgian, which is quintessential Greenwich style, you go up a gravel and Belgium-block driveway, passing huge lawns, grand trees, and horses standing in fields like garden ornaments.

The front door opens to a sweeping staircase rising up from a limestone floor. Off the entry, a hallway with barrel-vaulted ceilings and arched doors is decorated with antiques. At the end of the hall is a secretary; a wheel-back Regency chair can be used to sit in while writing a note. A colonnade of bell-jar lanterns light the ceiling, producing gorgeous reflections. Chippendale benches covered in needlework make an excellent place to sit and reflect on the view of the grounds.

The living room contains furniture collected by the client. Gilded scones flank a chinoiserie screen. The custom upholstered pieces are set against pale grass cloth walls. Some of the pieces were re-covered in English worn chintz from Colefax & Fowler; others were done in linen to effect an undecorated look. Tailored curtains with brush fringe finish the windows. The colors in the room are the same relaxed creams and greens used throughout the house.

The trellis-covered sunroom opens onto the vista beyond. I engaged opera set designer John Pascoe to create my image of a celadon gazebo with a blue sky. The room was hand-painted with lattice. Iron lanterns and sconces were used to create an illusion of being outside. Two "roundabouts" anchor the lanterns and act as sculptures in the center of the room.

The mix is what makes this room appealing. Painted furniture is combined with bamboo, iron planters, and stone garden consoles. Sisal rugs give the room a casual quality. The fabrics are all linens, which will only get better with time. The hint of gothic provided by the painted ivy bench reminds me of iron fretted work used on the tops of English greenhouses. Everyone loves discovering this unexpected room on the house's lower level. A "greenhouse" greets you at the bottom of the stairs. It's a great place to entertain next to the terraces outdoors.

At the top of the staircase, a hallway leads to the master bedroom. Halls are important because they connect, unify, and introduce the rooms beyond. At the end of the hall a window seat was added in a niche for sitting and writing while looking out onto the garden. The tea-stained vine fabric on the windows mimics the vines on the pergola outside.

My inspiration for this design was taken from the estate's grounds. It was important for me to marry the house's interior with the exterior. As a result, iron candlesticks and ivy-filled planters in the hall not only break up what could have been a long and unimaginative space but reflect the beauty of the property. I love the combination of the distressed cane chairs with the ornate gilt and stone console.

A well-traveled life is a part of Greenwich style. This home showcases collections—of photographs and rare crystal, to name two—found on memory-filled journeys. The collections remind the owners of times and places they have shared with family, friends, and loved ones.

Opposite and above: The relaxed creams and greens of the living room are used throughout the house.

Below: A sweeping staircase rises from the limestone floor.

*Iron lanterns and sconces in
the sunroom create the feeling
of being outdoors.*

The master bedroom is tranquil and serene. The celadon and cream color scheme is picked up from the hallway leading to the bedroom. The upholstered bed has a hand-painted cornice draped with cream linen and lined in sheers. The canopy is edged with cream and brush fringe, topped with wood beads. The pillows are embroidered in celadon with the couple's initials. I believe a bench or loveseat should always be at the foot of a bed. I had a craftsman in London make a velvet blanket chest topped with needlework. It's the ideal place to store an extra blanket or neck pillow.

I also like night tables to have shelves so there are books waiting at bedtime. The alabaster lamps on the night tables are adorned with pleated shades that give the room texture and light. A chaise in the corner is a terrific place to relax or make a phone call. Always have a throw or quilt nearby, or in your blanket chest.

My challenge with this house was to incorporate the client's furnishings into my design. I love the sunroom. I think everyone who lives in the country dreams of a solarium. I enjoyed working on the room with my talented friend, John Pascoe. It's remarkable how he can go from designing formidable opera sets for such stars as Placido Domingo to helping me create the perfect, modest-sized space for quiet solitude in a home, as we did for my client here.

The trellis-covered sunroom was
designed to evoke a gazebo with
a blue sky.

Opposite: A hallway leading to the master bedroom is decorated in vine fabric and ivy-filled planters to reflect the beauty of the property.

Above and left: The master bedroom offers comfort and serenity.

A Home of Distinction

A bay of windows in the living room creates an inviting and bright sitting area.

D riving up North Street—the Park Avenue of Greenwich—you turn into a private enclave, and at the end of a line of houses, past two stone pillars, stands an incredible new mansion. It's hard to tell the estate was not pre-war because the gardens and landscape trick you into believing the home has been there for years. In fact, the house, a Tudor English manor with a slightly modern edge, was built less than fifteen years ago.

The entry has richly detailed mahogany woodwork that is carried throughout the house. The distinctive octagonal entry features an antique Aubusson rug with colors that are used throughout the house just like the woodwork. The hand-painted chests, with hand-carved swag details, were commissioned from a craftsman in Maryland. I added the gilded mirrors. From her various travels, the client found the chow horse and chinoiserie dishes that dress the consoles.

The living room contains several seating areas. A bay of windows has a swag and jabot detailed treatment, which features rich woven trims, rosettes, and cords. The contrasting rose lining adds interest against the room's mahogany trim. The room is a series of windows so I purposefully made the walls and the window treatments in a similar tone to create a unified and unbroken background.

For one seating area, I used a curve-backed sofa in front of a bay of windows. Silk and Aubusson pillows decorate the sofa. A pair of Regency chairs, flanking a hand-painted tray table, make the corner inviting. This is a good place to sit and look out onto the gardens. When they are in bloom in the spring, the room feels

Books, photographs, and antique boxes are on display in the mahogany-paneled library.

like an extension of the outdoors. The rug, made by a French carpet company, was imported by Stark Carpets of New York. The colors echo those of the rug in the entry; the design was an archival Aubusson pattern I had reproduced.

Next to the living room is a mahogany-paneled library. Libraries are among my favorite spaces to design. Here I mixed wool paisley with a chenille sofa, leather chairs, and a needlepoint rug to make a comfortable place in which to read or sit by the fire. A tortoiseshell lampshade and leopard pillow were used for effect. The shelves are filled with books, framed photographs, and antique boxes purchased on the client's travels.

The dining room features a stunning Charles Winston chandelier. Off the dining room, a breakfast room has, at the client's request, a hint of country French. I added an iron lantern that fits nicely into the bay. I imported the chairs from France; they are displayed around a rectangular iron-based table. I bought the etching at the Trowbridge Gallery in London. A reproduction Aubusson rug gives the client the French feel she wanted.

Distinctive furnishings give this home character and quality.

At the top of the stairs, a landing is dressed with an embroidered table skirt with long bullion fringe. A gilded French chair flanks the table. The chinoiserie lamp has a pleated shade with tassel fringe.

The client wanted the bedroom belonging to her grown son, located on the second floor, to have an unusual acid-green color; I had the walls glazed to match her request. I added the four-poster British Colonial bed and night tables. I bought the tea canister lamps in London.

I love dark shades on lamps in dark rooms. These green silk pleated shades complement the lamps. A starburst mirror is framed between the posts of the bed. In the corner of a bedroom, there should always be a comfortable chair. This tufted silk chenille chair fits perfectly in the corner. I like maps and use them often; they work in almost any home.

Down the hall is another landing that leads to the daughter's bedroom. An antique English console table is placed outside her room. Above the table is one of the owner's favorite oil paintings, which she found with her daughter on a family trip to France. The painting provides a fond memory for both of them to view daily.

Left: The dining room features a Charles Winston chandelier.

Opposite: The breakfast room has a hint of country French.

In the daughter's room, the only place for the bed was in front of the window—it was the only wall in the room against which a queen bed could fit—so I created a half canopy as a backdrop for the carved upholstered French headboard. A chair rail was added to the room, and the walls were glazed a warm teal. A border and gold star paper were used on the ceiling, which makes the room feel feminine. The embroidered linens are the finishing touch.

Looking out from this room is a view of the grounds and pool, which is hidden between trees. The trees and boxwoods frame an English Lutyen's bench.

This home may be less than fifteen years old, but it looks and feels much older. Greenwich style reflects character and quality. Any house, no matter the age, can embrace Greenwich style. Some of my favorite properties I've designed have been new classics, as exemplified by this distinctive home.

Opposite: The son's bedroom is painted acid green, with antique maps on the wall.

Above: The daughter's bedroom has a half-canopy and an upholstered French headboard.

The gardens and landscape make this relatively new house feel much older. The pool is hidden between trees.

A Gentleman's Estate

The doors open to a curved staircase and walls lined with antique maps.

You might think designing for a designer is hard, but in many ways it's easier. Used to making snap decisions, designers are open-minded about other people's ideas, plus they understand form and style. In Tommy Hilfiger's case, he loves a classic look to his home. This is a man who is all about collections. He creates them and he owns them—cars, watches, maps, Warhols.

Because he is so creative, the design process ends up being one nonstop whirlwind of ideas that proceeds at a breakneck pace. In Tommy's world, everything needs to be done yesterday. But his excitement is so intense that his energy becomes infectious. That energy, I believe, is why he is so successful. I'm lucky because Tommy and I really enjoy working together; I've decorated eight homes for him.

Arriving at Tommy's back-country estate through private gates, you pass stone walls and white picket fences. The expansive lawns are groomed to perfection. A classic Belgium-block driveway features bronze urns and stately boxwoods. The garage has the feel of a carriage house except with a twist—a jaw-dropping collection of exotic cars. Outside, the house is pure Greenwich. Inside, it's classic, but with a touch of rock 'n' roll. Then again, what would you expect when you enter the home of Tommy Hilfiger?

As the door opens, you walk in to see a curved staircase dressed with custom houndstooth carpet—a reference to classic menswear suiting, an obvious reference for Tommy. The staircase runner is bound with nickel stair rods, a departure from traditional brass rods; this gives the staircase a modern yet timeless feel. The walls

The house is a classic with a touch of rock 'n' roll.

are covered in raffia; the floor is made of honed limestone with mahogany-colored stone keys. A black and white marble floor would have been expected; what you get is the unexpected, which is always a more interesting design choice. Instead of a usual brass lantern, I chose a unique mahogany fixture to give this soaring entry a sense of scale and balance.

On the entry walls, I displayed samples from Tommy's extensive antique maps collection, which he has been amassing for twenty years. At the top of the stairs, as a contrast to the more conservative maps, I hung selections from Tommy's extraordinary collection of autographed, black and white classic rock photographs, those whose subjects range from Jimi Hendrix to Mick Jagger to Janis Joplin. In a way they are as historic as the antique center hall table on which I displayed a hand-carved wooden American eagle.

The blend of styles is what makes this entry distinct. In keeping with classic style, I opted for tortoiseshell blinds, which prevent the area from feeling overdressed. On a buying trip in New York, I found a pair of antique bamboo consoles; I combined them with two mahogany star mirrors. The mirrors suggest Tommy's love of Americana—a theme that will become more evident in the house itself. A classic well-worn leather wing chair gives the entry a relaxed feel. Then, once again, the unexpected—Andy Warhol's Marilyn hovering beside it. In turn, an antique gilt American eagle contrasts with the Marilyn.

To me, this is the heart of Greenwich style: having the conviction to know what you like. Not being afraid to combine many styles into a look that works is the foundation on which I have built my design philosophy. With Tommy, that style is evident as soon as you walk in his front door.

The living room is tailored and refined, comfortable but unimposing. The room has two seating areas. Opposite a wall of French doors leading out to the swimming pool is one seating area. Here the English Bridgewater-style sofa is covered in linen. The end tables are antique black leather trunks with brass nail heads that were found in an antique shop in London; the trunks are piled with art books and leather and tortoise boxes. The chair, in a Bridgewater style as well, is covered in leopard from a fabric line designed by Rose Cummings, the groundbreaking American designer from the early twentieth century. An always-appropriate antique Louis Vuitton steamer trunk is used as a cocktail table. Sitting on top of a zebra rug, the trunk serves to anchor the room. Still, layering is what gives the room depth. The zebra skin rug lies on top of a custom wool, flat-weave rug.

As with other spaces in the house, two focuses of this room are the texture of materials and Tommy's ever-changing art collection. On the side chair, linen pillows are meant to accent the chair's animal fabric, just as the animal-print pillows enliven the sofa's plain covering. Still, nothing is meant to compete with the art. A Warhol Howdy Doody dominates the sofa; a Warhol shoe collage print looms in a corner behind the side chair. All of Tommy's Warhols are limited-edition lithographs, numbered and signed by the artist.

Over the fireplace, around which a second seating area is designed, artwork is "placed," not hung—a Warhol photograph of Mick Jagger, signed by both Warhol and Jagger, sits in front of a round wood-framed mirror—contributing to the room's layered effect. The color scheme and the slipper chairs, angled toward one another in front of the fireplace, evoke a vision of rooms once created by Billy Baldwin.

A legendary designer whose designs were classic but innovative, Baldwin was known for his brown and white rooms—clean and stylish, with a little kick, like

The living room blends linens with
animal prints, antiques with Warhols.

leopard or animal prints. His work would still be appropriate today. When I was a young girl, my mother gave me a book about Baldwin's designs, which I keep in my office even now. I often refer to it subconsciously when I design; in that way, Billy Baldwin has become a perpetual point of reference in my professional life.

Tommy's living room has a luxurious feel to it. The art is sensual and evocative. The fabrics, a combination of cashmere, leopard, and suede, are lavish and soft. Mixing things you love to create a personal space—that is another one of my goals in designing. This room is edgy, in part because of the mixture of textures and styles, yet it projects an aura of richness.

Off the living room is a mahogany-paneled library. The focus of the room is the linen sofa welted in saddle leather, which sits on an antique Herez rug layered over sisal matting. A Warhol Uncle Sam hangs over the sofa. Facing the sofa from the opposite wall is a fireplace. Displayed on the mantel is a framed American flag, which is fitting for Tommy since he often uses the American flag both in his designs and in the imaging for his company. These two pieces of Americana—a Warhol and an American flag—create an intriguing, but appealing, contrast.

A pair of Hermes-style tea canister maps creates the unique accent color to the library. Barcelona chairs are the right scale and add a sense of modern tradition. A humidor is tucked into the library shelves for those late-night discussions over brandy. A lounge chair with a cashmere throw sits next to the fireplace. A touch of cashmere against the suede armchair sitting on top of an old, worn rug—this is Greenwich style.

Every home needs a place for the family to gather. In the past, that area was called the "gathering" room, and it was a space, often located near the kitchen, where people assembled at mealtime to talk over the day's events.

The client was not afraid to mix styles, creating a distinct look.

Nowadays, we have renamed the area the "great" room. Not much has changed except the name. For Tommy, his great room is influenced by his trips out West and, once again, by his Warhols, specifically John Wayne and Buffalo Bill, which are displayed above the windows.

A remarkable stag-horn chandelier was custom made for the room by a craftsman in Colorado. The shed-horn chairs—from Crystal Farm in Colorado—are works of art themselves. They are reminiscent of a French Bregere chair, only in horn. The pony skin covering gives the chairs an unmistakable Western touch. The extra-large sofa coupled with two chaises produces an inviting space where the family can snuggle up and enjoy a fire in the massive fieldstone fireplace or simply watch television. The woven leather ottoman acts as a footrest as well as a cocktail table.

Scale is important in a room this enormous. The furniture must be in proportion to the room's height and width; here furnishings have to be large or they will be dwarfed by the room's size. Capping off the room—and taking advantage of its ample space—is a baby grand piano.

A first-floor guest room is heavily influenced by Tommy's love of Americana. Sailing flags and American flags form the room's defining theme; nautical antiques dress the bookshelves. The walls are glazed the color of faded denim, and the canvas-striped window treatments are headed with grommets and sailing cords. Stars and stripes dominate the room's decor. What could be more ageless than red, white, and blue? And more appropriate for Tommy Hilfiger?

The source of Tommy's passion for Americana is simple. He loves being American. After all, his is a true Horatio Alger story: small-town boy from upstate New York goes to Manhattan and ends up building an empire. Tommy adores all that the American flag stands for, which is why it is the symbol of his company and why it is a signature image in his homes.

The master bedroom returns to the theme of using a neutral backdrop to display personal memorabilia and art. Two of Tommy's favorite art pieces are here: a Warhol Jackie and another photograph of Mick Jagger. In fact, these pieces are the first objects visible upon entry to the room, but they blend in with family photographs in antique silver frames. The room's curtains are cream cashmere— simple, tailored, refined. In front of the window is a desk on which sits a grouping of antique watches,

Above and right: Monogrammed hangers and slippers are the kind of details found in this designer's home.

Opposite: The neutral colors of the master bedroom allow the artwork and memorabilia to stand out.

A bedroom reflects a love of Americana and a passion for collecting.

pens, and monogrammed stationery. A shell from Tommy's estate in Mustique is a subtle reminder of his home away from home.

The suggestion of influences from travels or places you love can easily be incorporated in your interiors as long as they do not become too literal. Your home should reflect the environment it is in, not some other place, so you should place an object only here or there to suggest favorite memories of other locations. The point is not to imitate another locale, but to allude to it carefully, as this room does.

The master bedroom overlooks the expansive grounds and pool. The navy canvas umbrellas echo those found at a beach resort. The classic white outdoor furniture is upholstered in navy canvas with white piping. There is an outdoor grill. The large Hilfiger family often gathers here for barbecues or entertaining. The lawn may be manicured, but it is sometimes used for tented parties or, much more frequently, tag football games.

All in all, while this home is a new classic, it also represents Greenwich style. It has a sense of history, but that history is as much about Jackie O and Mick Jagger as it is about antique maps. Greenwich style takes what in some cases may merely be timely—a piece of furniture, a photograph, an accent object—and, used properly in a suitable context, makes it classic and lasting.

Country Elegance

To many, a house in Greenwich is a retreat, an experience of being at home in the country. These houses do not look overdecorated, but lived in and loved. The style is relaxed, ready to create memories and family traditions.

A Country House

Above: Pillows on a bench give the entry warmth.

Opposite: A second entry is warmed by the light from English tole canister lamps.

Overleaf: The family spends most of its time in the kitchen, breakfast room, and family room.

From a distance, this house is stunning with its fieldstone facade, much of it covered by ivy. The house is accented by tall trees; in the middle of horse country, it's also surrounded by fields and fences. When you open the front door and walk in the entry, you discover a casual space defined by mahogany trim. I had the entry's carpet runner made in a rich red, ocher, and moss-green color scheme. Etched bell-jar lanterns create an appealing glow. Since there is no fabric in the entry, a bench is adorned with pillows to give it interest and warmth. The bench provides a place to sit while you take off your coat.

A second entry features an eighteenth-century center hall table, a great place to stack art books or display accent pieces. A pair of reproduction consoles enlarges the hall; English tole canister lamps with pleated silk shades sit on the consoles. I love lamplight. Its warm ambient glow is so attractive. I avoid using recessed lighting as much as I can. I prefer lanterns and sconces; they are more flattering and original to a house of this character.

The powder room was inspired by a faux bamboo painted chest I found in London. I added a wood back splash and, instead of using a sink, placed a wash-basin on it. The walls were upholstered. With a small bath, instead of trying to make it feel larger, I go with the fact that it's small and make it cozy and detailed. The antique mirror was found at a local auction.

The dining room is decorated in a moss-green stried paint. Since the ceilings are low, everything, including the base and crown, is done in the same dark green.

Opposite: The faux-painted mantel gives the dining room a relaxed, country look.

Above: Adjacent to the dining room is a sunroom, which has an antique wine rack and rattan coffee table.

The ceiling was papered in a parchment star wall covering. When I'm working with a low ceiling, I do not ignore it; I embrace it. The client owned the dining room furniture. I reupholstered it and placed it in the context of an appealing environment. The interesting detail in the room is the mantel I had faux-painted in a pine finish. The mantel was originally a plain, white-painted wood—it had been added by the previous owner—but I chose to paint it in a style that would offer a more relaxed, country look. Now it looks like a great antique piece. The curtains are a red and green linen; tassels of woven bells were added to the edge, and the lining is a small red and green plaid.

I used traditional furnishings with casual elements throughout the house. Instead of flowers on the dining table, I used fruits, vegetables, and ivy. Things do not have to be "important" to be beautiful, if done creatively. There were bookcases in the room; I added an antique mirror so they would sparkle at night yet still complement the age of the house. The room is a pure joy when the red tole lantern is lit and the fireplace is blazing.

A nearby sunroom doubles as a sitting room for the first-floor guest room. The space feels more like a sunroom because of the faux bamboo trellis ceiling paper. Casual diamond-pattern sisal was used with the wide-board floors. A mix of

upholstery, country French chairs, and a rattan cocktail table makes the room unique. I found the wine rack at an antique sale on the local green in Bedford, New York; it seemed right for the house. Found pieces can give personality to a room, as the wine rack does here. The doors in the room were left unadorned and open to a terrace for entertaining. The room provides a great place to read the newspaper in the morning or to have drinks before dinner.

The mudroom-hallway is one of my favorite places in the house. Never overlook a hallway. It is too vital a space; it leads to the rest of the house—the country kitchen, in this case. The hall opens to a small courtyard with one of the best views in the house. I transformed the hall into a potting room with a rustic table and flowerpots. The wicker furniture and botanical screen give the house another "room," instead of another hallway. What a great place to arrange flowers or to leave your "Wellies."

The library is the ultimate country retreat. All of the woodwork and bookcases have been glazed a merlot red against upholstered plaid walls. The curtains are a hunting-dog toile, which complements the bold red plaid. The mantel has been faux-finished in mahogany. It instantly creates age and richness and makes the mantel the room's focal point. The needlepoint rugs and eclectic furnishings feel as if they have been collected over the years, which adds to the warmth of the room. This is where the family relaxes or where they take their guests after dinner to sit next to a roaring fire.

The house has a wonderful kitchen with a breakfast room bay and adjoining family room. This area is a gathering place for the family. With stone floors, wood beams, iron lanterns, and warm fabrics, the rooms look out onto beautiful landscaped terraces and horse fields. The family spends most of their time here, and it is a great place for casual entertaining.

This house does not look overdecorated, but lived in and loved. It has an understated elegance, yet will make anyone feel welcome. I'm pleased with the design of the house, a property that has afforded me the ultimate compliment paid to a designer. Once I had finished my work, the clients lived in the house for a time, then sold it. Two buyers bid on it. The new owners made major changes in the decor, kept the house for a while, then, because they had to relocate, put the house up for sale. This time, the previous opposing bidders snapped it up and hired me to restore it to the way it looked when they first saw it. They had loved my design so much when they tried to buy the house the first time they wanted me to restore my original design, which I was thrilled to do.

Opposite: The living room is a combination of traditional furnishings and casual elements.

Above: The bathroom was designed around a faux-bamboo chest found in London.

A Mountain Retreat

*S*everal of my clients have second, even third homes that I have been lucky enough to decorate. There is nothing more wonderful than being able to leave your "normal" life and relax in a place where you are allowed to unwind and live the other life you have always dreamed of. Every time I go to Vail or Verbier, I dream of "checking out" to become a ski instructor, even if I know I could never leave my true passion of designing.

The client who owns this house called and made one of the most gentlemanly requests I have ever heard. He began by saying he was thinking about buying his wife a ski house as a surprise Christmas present. Since she had had three children in less than five years, he didn't want to give her the burden of decorating a new house. Because he loved what I had done with their Greenwich home, he wanted to know if I could decorate their weekend house but keep it a secret from his wife. I loved the romance—and the challenge—of the idea.

I started with the architectural plan of the house he bought and turned it into a mountain retreat. This home is beautiful at all times of the year—from summer to autumn to winter. What's great about designing a home that is not your main home is that it allows you the freedom of doing more amusing things. I searched the markets for taxidermy bears, Adirondack-style pieces, and anything made of stag horn. I traveled to auctions, antique shows, and stores in ski locations in Colorado, Vermont, and out West. I wanted to accumulate pieces that would give the house character.

A stag mirror in the entry welcomes visitors to this mountain retreat.

The entry creates an instant statement that says you are in another world—a mountain escape. Incredible details were created here, such as the twig-and-birch-bark chair rail. A bronze stag mirror complements the tramp art console, all against a tartan backdrop.

In the living room, the colors are warm. The furniture is comfortable; it will only get better with age. The mix of wool plaids, bronze bears, leather, twig, and stag transports you to that "weekend place" state of mind. The huge leather and wood plank cocktail table is almost six feet long; it's a good place to rest your feet after a long day on the slopes. When the fire is lit, there is no more inviting place to cuddle up with a loved one than the nearby sofa, under a fur throw.

I had the rug in the living room produced in China, where it was aged and worn to make it look like an original. Artisans were brought in to create details such as the twig wainscot in the powder room. Every element in the house looks as if it just happened; in fact, my massive treasure hunt lasted more than six months before I had accumulated all of the pieces I wanted. Attention to detail was a priority. From the leather couches to the snowshoe sconces—no detail was ignored. The massive stone fireplace and the hand-hewed beams give the house a timeless feel, one that suggests the house will provide memories for generations to come.

The walls are painted a camelhair color to blend with the pine beams and woodwork. Nothing looks contemporary; every effort was made to insure that all of the room's elements looked aged. I made sure none of the furnishings were too fragile, for this was a place to kick back and to worry about nothing more than the sheer joy of escape.

Comfortable furniture, warm colors, and a mix of materials make the living room a perfect place to relax.

One of the most enjoyable events associated with skiing comes when the day is over and everyone gathers to cook a meal. In this house the dining room is big enough to accommodate a crowd but still cozy enough for a family to have a quiet breakfast. I had a designer make the special hand-carved chandelier with skin shades and stag heads reminiscent of Bavarian black forest pieces. The clock is present to make sure no one misses the early morning lift; it is in the Black Forest motif. Old Hickory created the woven chairs, which have woven backs and leather seats. The wool curtains are hung on birch bark poles but are detailed with suede tabs and horn buttons.

This house has the ultimate country kitchen. The dark green cabinets look amazing against the pine woodwork and white plank floors. The island's top was designed in wood to give it a less "kitchen" feel. The island acts as a buffet piece and large table. The twig-and-birch-bark detail was added to the kitchen hood. The entire room was warmed by the camel-colored walls and ceiling. The light fixtures I had specially made for this kitchen out of iron with a flanking deer motif and mica shades. The stools have different animals in pressed metal and are made of iron and leather so they can take a beating from kids and an occasional ski boot. Who wouldn't love to prepare a Thanksgiving dinner here?

The library features pine paneling and leather wing chairs as well as a stone fireplace and custom twig chairs. It's a comfortable place to sit and read by the fire.

There are six bedrooms and one huge bunkroom with six bunks. The master bedroom is enticing with its view of the lifts. I had the four-poster twig-and-birch-bark bed designed to accommodate the peaked ceiling. I mixed fur and needle-point pillows, found in London, with "Horchow" wool patchwork quilts. The curtains are richly detailed with nail heads and chenille fan-edge trim. The texture is

Opposite: Light fixtures with flanking deer and mica shades were specially made for the kitchen.

Left: The deer motif appears again in the stag-head chandelier in the dining room.

like a flannel blanket, layered over wood blinds. A custom needlework rug was created for the space; it's set atop a wool high-low sisal rug.

Two of the children's rooms are particularly fun. The daughter's has a white willow and reed bed with a patchwork quilt. The braided rug in rose and green is reminiscent of old Vermont hook rugs but more practical. The walls were painted a sage green to make the lofty room more cozy and intimate. In contrast, the boy's room has a unique bunk bed I designed with a full bed on bottom and a twin bed on top. This bed is covered in flannel blankets and sheeting and a bear fur throw. The bear theme was taken from a fabulous chenille fabric I used on the curtains. A blue and tan palette is used throughout. I kept the room fun yet handsome by using tailored detailing and nail heads so that the son wouldn't outgrow it.

If you are in Vermont, your home should feel like Vermont, like the retreat it should be. But you can carry Greenwich style with you wherever you go. Representational of who you are and the way you live your life—that's Greenwich style. Greenwich style may be suggestive of a real place in Connecticut, but it also implies a lifestyle, a value system, a way of looking at the world.

There are six bedrooms in the house,
all designed to keep family members
and guests comfortable.

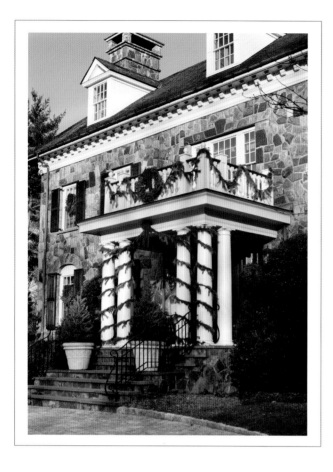

Home at the Holidays

This historic Greenwich estate is decorated at Christmastime with pines, berries, and a grand Christmas tree.

This stone manor house has been the setting for many a holiday celebration, from business parties to family gatherings. It's so stunning it has been on the Historical Society's tour of homes. Outside, the mahogany-shuttered windows are festively decorated with wreaths, while the portico and columns are swaggered with bows of pine, ready for the holiday season. The classic Connecticut estate, with its Belgium-block driveway and fieldstone front, is welcoming. The house's look is grand but always inviting.

The front door opens onto a staircase dressed for the holidays with magnolia leaf swags and berries. An English table with cut crystal hurricane lamps and antique boxes graces the entry. Depending on the season, the table is dressed in a variety of arrangements. At Christmas, a tortoiseshell vase is filled with pomegranates, pines, and berries. The pine-scented candles fill the room with the scent of the holiday season.

The table sits on a faux-bois floor designed so no rug is needed in the entry. The wood accents on the stair railings and mahogany doors contrast with the tones of the foyer floor. A Greek key-and-medallion border surrounds the foyer. The entry is treated as a room with a pair of Regency chairs, an antique table, and a bronze lamp. The area was covered in a hand-blocked Cole-and-Son English damask, which has a large enough scale to turn the huge entry into an intimate space. Eighteenth-century engravings of the four seasons grace the walls.

The entry's focal point is the view from the front door back to the dining room

Right: Regency chairs and an antique table make the entry feel like a room.

Opposite: The library is decorated in jewel tones from the antique Orient.

Overleaf: The library is designed around an eighteenth-century English bookcase with bronze grillwork.

window. The dining room has swagged silk curtains in reds, camel, and celadon; the walls are covered in Chinese wallpaper panels from Charles P. Gracie that have a camel background. The ceiling is not forgotten. It is papered in gold tea paper that glows in the light of the crystal chandelier and candlelight.

The English dining room table and chairs were found on a trip to London. The set sits on top of a Regency-style Aubusson rug. The open backs of the chairs create wonderful silhouettes. As grand as the dining room is, the colors are comfortable. The table is set with gilded chargers to complement the ceiling and dinnerware. Cut crystal hurricane lamps and stemware on monogrammed linen napkins add to the experience of being entertained in this stunning room. A Chippendale-style breakfront is lit to display a collection of English dinnerware and crystal stemware. The room is the epitome of gracious living; it evokes a timeless quality meant to be enjoyed by family and friends for generations, especially during the holidays.

The contrast between the entry and the mahogany-paneled library draws you in. The room is decorated in jewel tones taken from the antique Oriental. All the fabrics are chenilles and velvets, with a touch of silk accents. The pillows of challis paisley contrast with the silk damask beaded pillows. There is a mix of antique

Opposite: Mahogany pieces are used
throughout the house to balance the
doors and woodwork.

Above: The hand-carved mahogany
mantel is the centerpiece of the
living room.

and reproduction furniture in the room, but every piece was chosen to accentuate
the room's centerpiece—an eighteenth-century English bookcase with bronze
grillwork. A library does not have to be entirely "built in." It's more interesting to
design a room around a great piece of furniture, as I did here.

The bookcase is filled with antique leather-bound books. Shelves are only as
beautiful as what goes on them. Careful consideration should go into filling bookshelves and cabinets. Shelves can be filled with leather books, fossils, seashells, or
even art on easels. Etchings of ancient battle scenes, found in a map shop outside
of London, are used around the room to fill the paneled walls.

The living room opens onto a hand-carved mahogany mantel. Over the mantel
hangs one of the client's favorite Zimbari paintings. Another hangs over the sofa on
the opposite side of the room. The walls are glazed in a wheat-colored sties similar
to the background of the wallpaper used in the entry. This creates a flow from one
room into another. All of the woodwork is stippled a similar color, as is the ceiling.

The living room has several seating areas. A piano graces the alcove. A red chinoiserie secretary and a tall Tiffany clock help to balance the vastness of the room.
Mahogany pieces were used throughout to balance the doors and woodwork. The
combination of styles and collections gives the room a classic Greenwich style.

The informal section of the house was recently added in a major renovation.
An effort was made to blend the style of the addition with that of the original. The

The dining room is a stunning place to entertain yet is comfortable enough to be enjoyed by family and friends.

The kitchen and breakfast area are decorated lavishly during the holidays.

kitchen, which was also added, boasts pine-coffered ceilings and woodwork to make the space feel as if it had always been there. Clive Christian built the English pine cabinetry. The hearth over the stove is a good place to add swags at Christmastime; the island is big enough for several family members to use at once or for the children to spread out and do homework.

An iron and bronze chandelier lights the island. The challenge with the enormous size of the kitchen, which includes a breakfast area, was to make it feel homey. The client had chosen the window treatment fabric; I decided to make the walls a rich blue, which sets off the pine cabinets. The color took a large and imposing space and made it seem more intimate. At the holidays, the room is decorated lavishly, since the family spends most of its time here.

Off the kitchen, the great room is paneled in a darker version of the pine, with molding detail and an antique beamed ceiling. A vast fieldstone fireplace was designed to be seen from the kitchen. This room can accommodate a thirty-foot Christmas tree, which is displayed with all of the family's cherished ornaments.

The owners purchased the stag horn chandelier to remind them of their weekend home in Vermont. It provides light to the center of the lofty room. The curtains are on large rings and poles with long wood-bead trim. The room is meant to be enjoyed all year long but especially during the holidays.

The pine-paneled great room has
a stone fireplace and a stag-horn
chandelier, reminiscent of the family's
weekend home in Vermont.

I designed the master bedroom suite around a linen Colefax & Fowler fabric I used on the bed's canopy. The client had an affinity for Aubusson carpets, so I covered the floor in a pale wool sisal matting and layered the carpets on top of it. The client's existing bed was redesigned with a hand-painted tester to create a half canopy. The room was large, so it needed the volume of a tall object. A tester can give a feeling of graciousness, without requiring fabric on all four corners of the bed, which can obstruct the views of the fireplace or television.

The bench at the bottom of the bed is a nice place to sit in front of the fire. A collection of botanical prints covers the walls, and crystal lamps with smocked shades flank the bed. The room is a blend of mahogany furniture along with dark chinoiserie accents. I favor a touch of black in a room; it keeps a pastel palette from getting too sweet.

Above: The gentleman's bathroom has medallion wall coverings and is decorated with pieces the clients love.

Opposite: The sitting room off the master bedroom is a blend of mahogany furniture and dark chinoiserie pieces.

Overleaf: The bed was designed with a hand-painted tester and half canopy of linen Colefax & Fowler fabric.

The sitting room has a custom-designed armoire that houses clothing as well as a television. There are some small-scale pieces to make the children feel at home when they are visiting their parents. The sitting room overlooks the garden below. I added garden elements, which look wonderful against the floral linens. A rose and celadon silk-stripe curtain was selected for the bay window; it is a companion to the glazed wall color. The light on this side of the house can get harsh, so I layered sheers under the curtains to soften the brightness.

The client loves toile. The walls in the shared dressing area were covered in a pale rose toile covering. Another Aubussan runner covers the floor, and lanterns were added to the ceiling to give the room a colonnade effect. This brings soft, ambient light to the dressing hall.

When the house was bought, the gentleman's bathroom had a strange mica tile that seemed out of place. Instead of discarding it, I added a tea paper ceiling to give the same reflection as the tiles. The medallion wall covering complements the tile and stone, and a celadon and brown window treatment was added over wood blinds.

Always take care in decorating your bathroom. Make the space warm and personal with monogrammed towels, cherished art, and pieces you love. Your style should not stop at the public places. It should be carried out in spaces throughout your home.

This house is the ultimate place to gather a family during the holidays. There are lots of guest rooms for people to sleep over and plenty of places for the children to play. Decorating for the holidays is the time to create traditions. Every time you take down the box of Christmas ornaments, it brings fond memories of your childhood. It's reminiscent of your family, of good times spent with the people you love. If nothing else, Greenwich style is about traditions—making them and keeping them.

Acknowledgments

My appreciation and heartfelt thanks go to so many. Writing a book is similar to the practice of interior design. A project could never happen without the talent and dedication of a team of artists, as well as the trust of wonderful clients.

First, I would like to thank the clients who have given me the pleasure of being part of their homes and their lives. I am grateful for their patience when we had to disrupt their households with stylists and photographers to create the beautiful pictures in this book. I hope the experience was not too much of a burden and that they will all enjoy seeing their homes on these pages.

This book was just a concept when I ran the idea past my friend and client, Tommy Hilfiger. Tommy has always been very supportive and convinced me that indeed this book should be done. For all his advice and inspiration, I am sincerely grateful.

I thank Rizzoli and my publisher, Charles Miers, for giving me the opportunity to create this book. I enjoyed so much working with Alex Tart, my editor. She was so helpful in making the book happen. She also suggested the very talented book designer Abigail Sturges, who turns every photograph and word into a work of art.

My gratitude goes to all of our talented photographers for their discerning eyes and beautiful images. Thanks to Nancy Hill, Michael Partenio, Kit Kittle, Tom McWilliam, and his assistant, Michel Leroy. And to stylist Corey Tippen, Ben Diep, and his assistant in photo printing, Gary Guan.

My personal love and appreciation go to Roger Faynor, who throughout the years has always been able to interpret fabric into the most beautiful creations and who, most importantly, puts up with our insane deadlines.

To Paul Alexander, the night owl who helped me get through this project with his words and experience. I appreciate all he has done to contribute to my first venture in the publishing world.

Thanks also to Bobbi Eggers for her inspiration early on, as well as her understanding and thoughtfulness.

My regards and thanks to Peter Saverine and Callie Craumer at Colony Florist for being there with flowers at a moment's notice. And to Wendy Seagal at Greenwich Orchids for her beautiful bouquets.

To everyone at Rinfret Ltd. and Rinfret Home & Garden who assisted me with their inspiration and patience. They have all worked so diligently and carried on while I have been out on photo shoots. My appreciation goes to Barbara Fibak Olszewski, whose beautiful drawings allow me to create my concepts, and to my dedicated and delightful design assistants, Marisa Bistany, Christine Griffiths, and Stacy Tarfano. Thanks to the important ladies who keep everything accountable and in order: Joanne Zawalski and Sue Neil. Thanks also to Hillary Merrill, Kem Moran, and Kim Weiner, who keep Rinfret Home & Garden beautiful and the designers and clients happy.

Very special recognition goes to Amy Adianis Hirsch, who always amazes me with her dedication and talent, and who continues to enjoy the design business as much as I do. She inspires me daily, and I think of her as my kindred spirit.

And to Steven Autry, who has my sincere admiration and gratitude. He has such great style, enthusiasm, and talent. Steven always makes everything look incredible and is a joy to work with, whether in the shop on buying trips or organizing photography. He kept me focused on getting this book finished, and I could not have done it without his smile, sense of humor, and support.

A special thank you to my mother, Kathleen Sikorski, who taught me early on about design, style and the importance of creating a beautiful home. And to my brothers, Patrick and Brian, who have always been there to encourage me.

Finally, and most of all, my love goes to my husband, Peter, and my children, Spencer and Taylor, who have always been my source of happiness in a somewhat hectic life. I apologize for dragging them to antique shows, photo shoots, and my office on far too many weekends and evenings. I dedicate this book to you with all my gratitude and affection. You are my inspiration in everything I do.

To all, my sincere thanks
CINDY RINFRET

Photography Credits